Error and Angels

Publication of this book was supported by a grant from the Eric Mathieu King Fund of The Academy of American Poets.

THE James DICKEY

CONTEMPORARY POETRY SERIES

EDITED BY RICHARD HOWARD

Error and Angels

Poems by

Maureen Bloomfield

UNIVERSITY OF SOUTH CAROLINA

Published in Columbia, South Carolina, by the
University of South Carolina Press

Manufactured in the United States of America

01 00 99 98 97 5 4 3 2 1

Library of Congress Cataloging-in-Publication Data

Bloomfield, Maureen, 1950–
Error and angels : poems / by Maureen Bloomfield.
p. cm. — (The James Dickey contemporary poetry series)
ISBN 1–57003–193–2 (CL). — ISBN 1–57003–194–0 (PB)
I. Title. II. Series.
PS3552.L63967E7 1997
811'.54—dc21 97–4724

For J, K, and M

Contents

III

A Note on Maureen Bloomfield

The makings of this new poet, so ardent yet so verecund, are not about religion: they are about the *difficulties* of religion, the hampering of devotional impulse and the problematics of the gestures and the sentiments of worship without a community, without even a ceremony to abide in, to abide by. So the voice in these contraverted orisons is always *in solitary,* though not confined, rather wandering, on the loose, and seeking, actually, lodging. Such habitation is to be found, it would seem, in art best of all, by the waiting catechumen. I am deliberately employing the vocabulary of divine service, in part because Ms. Bloomfield makes such use of it ("And thus desire is better / if it remains a prayer," she remarks with a certain shrewdness), and in part because I want to emphasize the ecstatic commitment of these frequently ecphrastic addresses: to Giorgione's "Tempesta," to Leonardo's "Annunciation," to the pre-Raphaelite Henry Holliday's "Meeting of Dante and Beatrice," to some "Birth of the Virgin," probably Lorenzetti's, though she will not specify, and to the ambiguous stained-glass walls of Sainte-Chapelle ("love / is unendurable"). Just listen to the obstacles placed in the way of adoration:

> . . . Too early for the Uffizi,
> we creep into Santa Maria Novella and interrupt a Mass.
> The cavernous *chiesa* is aglow with votive candles
> that a stocking-capped old woman sells, in the foyer,
> from a box, and the murmurous hum of women
> praying for their apostate sons. . . .

That's what the church is aglow with: prayers for apostate sons. And the poet proceeds down her *via negativa,* after some harrowing details among the visitors:

> The Golden Gate hardly matters, except
> in the retelling. It isn't gold at all.

The proper attitude toward reverence is, evidently, one of reversal, cancellation, erasure even. There is a direction to the reader of *Error and Angels* in Ms. Bloomfield's tight-lipped but telling Notes: "The collection's title invokes John Donne's poem 'Air and Angels.'"—Invokes, yet deliberately distorts, a celebrated scholastic doctrine explaining why an angel has "Face and wings / of air, not pure as it, yet pure": in order to appear to men, angels assumed bodies of air which were pure but not as pure as the angelic essence. Donne's aporia ("just such disparity / as is 'twixt air and angels' purity") is nowhere near negative enough for this poet, who chooses to underhear, as it were, the famous title as, typically, "Error and Angels," as though it would be error, not air, that the divine messenger must assume in order to be apprehensible to us.

There is a kind of relief among these backward fervors (there has to be: the poet knows just how to administer her homely details, the domestic heft that keeps us with her, sustains the utterance on a bearable plane amid so much that is tormented, withheld, denied), a respite in these intensely observed *scenes:*

> Back home in Cincinnati, the right-to-lifers parade,
> like pages trailing ticker tape, on the stock market's floor,
> only they are fat and poor, these presidents of Holy Name clubs—
> in T-shirts and ball caps, pushing strollers. Before
> the court injunction they would crouch behind a planter, then
> spring,
> when a young girl, as in the Presentation, would mount the
> Jacob's
> ladder to the clinic's portico. . . .

Indeed, how often the glamorless Catholicism of writers like J. F. Powers and Flannery O'Connor is worked into the texture of the poetry here as a kind of remorseless contrast (between the Renaissance splendors and the Ohio drears), but also an insistent identification:

> the musk young girls give off, as they stir,
> tossing twists of heavy hair, in church, say,
> like Beatrice or Laura, turning to find
> their missals in the pew and the boys behind them
> who are breathless, rapt, and because they are
> *out of time*, inevitably mistaken.

She is a hard one, this onlooker at the laying-out: "Smoothed over her twiggy body was a pink / chiffon nightgown she could only have been caught dead in," and that is her grace, even her Grace: *hard-won.* I am in awe of such consecrations.

Richard Howard

Acknowledgments

I am grateful to the editors of the publications in which the following poems first appeared:

The Cincinnati Poetry Review
"Dies Irae"

The Kenyon Review
"Street Songs (I, II, III)"

The New Republic
"Lotto"

The Paris Review
"La Grande Châsse"
"Postulant"

Shenandoah
"Rock and Tree and Water"
"The Wood of Error"
"To Be Childless Is an Error?"

The Southern Review
"The Meeting of Dante and Beatrice"

Western Humanities Review
"Y W H"
"Charing Cross"

PART I

The Wood of Error

Midway in life, I woke alone in a third floor bedroom,
My breath rank within the hood of blankets—
Alone in a wilderness arduous and cold: the night air

Of contemplative October, the attic quarter windows—
And I saw the leopard of the gaudy poems, the lion
Of the need to die, circling the sloped, brick walls,

And I turned on my stomach, curving in the flannel sheets
Wrapped tight around the box springs—our makeshift bed
Of coils where the she-wolf of the straw ribs springs

If I press down, seeking to be empty,
Where I can hear the swimmer in the mattress
Looking back, his eyes inflamed from brackish water

That had only seemed an azure calm,
And looking out the quarter windows, I saw, across on Vine,
Monroe's Avalon Gardens, the Miller High Life neon

Making the sidewalk yellow. Three women in felt hats
And a man in a cinched-in coat looked down;
At ease in their bodies, they talked of each other

In the future time, until I overheard
The intimate, the getting-ready, the pocketing of keys,
And their voices, rising like the forced, hot air—O Lady

Of Permutations, quit your complaining,
Stop that circling round, just come,
O Mama, just come over here

Street Songs

Above the cliff's last rise we reached in time
An open slope. "Do we go right or left,"
I asked my Master, "or do we still climb?"
Dante, Canto IV, *Purgatorio*

I. The View from Here

Too early for the hothouse, I park at the prospect
Of yellow frame and robin's egg houses: only one way
To totter, it seems now. But the radio's Honey Dipper

Says, *If you ain't goin' up, you goin' in—*
Into trouble, into misfortune, into sin. In a hurry,
The tourists in ski jackets check their watches,

Lest they surprise the forced blooms the gardener
Has buried in the dark. In the Honey Dipper's story,
An angel plucked once, from beneath his cloak of ashes,

A gold and then a silver key. "Saint Peter bade me err
In opening rather than in shutting out."
The guard unknots the lock. *Up and out, relax.*

Man, we'll all get in: Unity's
The way. The second, the silver
Key unfurls the road in daylight—requiring art.

II. The Dance

It's so hot, Death, his torso a rivulet of worms,
Is calling on the radio: *All the time I hear*
"I think this" or *"I think that . . . in my opinion. . . ."*

Let me tell you, brothers and sisters. You think
It matter what you think? What you better be
Askin' is "What do God know?" A red Corvette

Has set up shop outside Avalon Gardens-Bar
Where, with the bass's thrum, we're drawn.
The doorway is two lines—the deal:

Before the jive and after. *Man, not much*
Money in your pocket now. What's shit is shit.
You lookin' beautiful, Carlotta.

When he trails a breath across the record's floor
The Dipper draws a silver thread through sequin eyes.
In the sleepers' sides he plies the needle.

III. Memorials

The future's full of holes. Wishes
Leave, except in language, no traces.
Passage is a myth, the neighbors know.

They have swallowed the Irish Rose
And wait out the sacramental aftermath
Inside Fobb's Barber Shop, while the rain,

Immediate and imminent, insists a question
That requests a definition. But dough's
The mystery—not time, money: we know *what;*

We askin' *when* and *who.* Alongside stacked jars
Of tonic, barber chairs in rows—string ties
And headbands are clotted on a cardboard trestle.

No one even wants a haircut. Today's
Too late—to get a new "do" rained on. *Lookin' good*
Enough for yesterday and for tomorrow now.

IV. Lotto

It's an act not a prayer the prophet
Calls the world to. The calendulas
Are burnt enough already from the fever

On the street where traffic slows, shoulders
Out of cars, exchanging dreambook dreams
Mama knows the numbers of. You can divide

Or add: it depends on what you like, man,
The combinations, or the feel. The sounds
Should be on key, for instance, at tickwatch

Intervals, or echoing the refrigerator's hum.
And sometimes a beat should catch up and lap
The other, breaking stride. In the pony kegs

That smell of Lysol, sweet pastry is wrapped
To keep the night. "Baklava"—a good word
Seeped in nuts and dipped in honey. Three sounds

Three souls—you can save for later: what comes due
Tomorrow's a ticket in your pocket, if you spend,
If you waste, if you play the feeling now.

Rock and Tree and Water

I

An ancient painting never grows toward one direction,
The Chinese scholar said, but the days seem to collect
Like straight pins in a jar—becoming calculable overnight.

The contest: to estimate the number, a game combining
Chance and skill, for the winner would have to measure
Intervals by remembering that the property of gifts

Was that they be unlucky, before the cave blotted now
With ochre hands. Le Douanier blurred, once, handkerchiefs
For clouds, and Chinese emperors took the rocks for mountains.

Humility, the virtue of amateurs, must be insistence,
Something won—a way of looking, after all.

II

Sister Humilitas in a habit drawn in watery ink
Followed the children into the lavatory to warn:
The bolt of cotton toweling could catapult—

A waterfall—acne and fever from the clammy wall.
Once she must have thought herself too proud.
Her name chosen, she stood at the streaked blackboard,

And only the children thought her beautiful.
She limned the philodendron's leaves in clay,
Her words incommensurable, in a landscape without scale.

Distant mountains have no stones. And the mist
Evokes the soul, for in her resignation was her care,
And past the mountains, fishing boats in willows,

So was time, where we would love—
Alone in our judgments from that day.

Blessed Giuliana

Santissima Annunziata, Firenze

Someone must have thought a miracle would happen.
Available for intercession, conveniently exposed

In a glass case like a carry-out Sleeping Beauty—
No beauty, she. A thumb face presiding

Over the mendicant's habit, her dwindling body
Almost a column, as if she were a caryatid on its side.

In 1986, her cheeks look fuller than her picture
On the postcard from the holy-pictures store, as if

A dreaming sacristan had stuffed cotton like moons,
Force-feeding the anorectic hosts, or like her altar's

Painted crucifix, she had been, after the flood of 1966,
Reinterpreted, restored. Did a penitent waking to the crash

Of water save her then, when the Arno rushed waist-deep,
Staining the *pietra serena* with a caul of mud, or

Did she, in her bier plated with cherubim and dolphins,
Breathe, like Moses with a reed, above the water

Until coming to rest in the rushes of the pews,
Where I sit now—no Miriam, her only visitor

Reading the story hand printed on a placard:
Giuliana Falconieri, founding the Servite Order,

To relieve the burdens of the poor, "served God,"
And now, bearing a gilded lily, serves as her own

Principal mourner, having been efficacious in this life,
But not, it seems, hereafter. No ex-votos hang like Valentines,

But perhaps it was her choice: to disdain the pomp of miracles,
The adulation of the crowd. Alone all night in the cold vestibule—

Not even, like a parakeet, covered up—her enormous, sleeping
    head
Tells how the soul is visible through trial. Except in the *Blue Guide*

Which skips over her: after six hundred years, an embarrassment:
To have attained only the first step, beatitude—the bright hope

Given up: sainthood for a local girl. Too late to inter her
Next to Andrea del Sarto in the wall—a Lucrezia in reverse, adamant

(Del Fede), in her faith. Americans, too shy to laugh at Jesus as
An S-M star, take a jab at Giuliana: a joke on Catholicism, on Venus

Clothed, as if for reparation after rapture, on her couch. But every
Body is a reliquary: the numinous in its own box. She endures,

Exiled from the collegiality of celebrants, her trial—
Bereft of Magdalen, the Blessed Mother, John—as if doubt

Stored up like radium could assume, in its half-life,
Grace—with intercession always timely, ticking, coming up.

For it's not too late to be admitted to the wedding feast,
Though it will be hard to put on the silken cowl, to bow.

The future is no longer her objective, as if she were,
At last, too proud to be welcomed now.

Don't Borrow Trouble, Chil'

The pictures were hung salon-style—too close together,
As if they'd sprouted, like dug-up bulbs, stray wings
On the wall of palest mauve,
The stenciled tendrils as a border
For the good, if unspecific, time.

Though far from the muddy Ohio, that river
Cast a spell, even here in Chelsea,
Through the haze of Killer Dope. Stacks of review copies
And thumbed galleys did not betray
The constancy of dust. Ninth Avenue,

Like a river, had scattered
Fuchsia cars along its ridge. It seemed as though,
From this height, she could weigh the words
Like glitter, 40¢ an ounce, a handful from a jar.
The only woman at the party, she drew breath

And saw it furl into the windows of the poets' sides.
They did not mark her. Was it possession—a question of—
Singular or plural; the case derives from syntax:
What could she now use? In this state, the question was
Probably a mistake, as if overnight

The apostrophes had been driven from these
And from all the other words.

La Grande Châsse

When the Midwest sky is that old-clothes, cardboard
Color, and the hillsides are too visible,
In their poverty of intention, exposed,
I think, sometimes, of how you blocked
The future, as if it were a scene, and wrote it
In a letter before you drove all night through snow.

Twenty years after, I dream, and it is Sainte-Chapelle:
The out-of-bounds, the treacherous clerestory;
The vestibule's diminution, and
The rose window, cinereous in gloom.
So much, at last, I want to tell you! The story
Of the world, but it is night upon

The stained-glass windows of the wall. The virgin bows
And would be taken. Joseph wakes.
The nave is barred with lilies and with snow. *Love*
Is unendurable. She will not know him.
Joseph wakes, and at the angel's voice, he goes.

The Meeting of Dante and Beatrice

"Love is not consolation; it is light."
Simone Weil, *Notebooks*

Is this an image from a mirror, or the Ponte alle Grazie
From the Arno's other side, as in early morning
Dreams—a prophecy from Scipio, further
Than the second-hand boundary of the future's door.
Being, entrusted to recollection, is language,
The philosopher said, and thus enters
The historical, not history, exactly. The second best,
The flirt, throws her head back to get a better look
At the poet, his hand angled theatrically near his heart:
A sign to her who is proud and will not look, fearing

The future that he will say he knows.
Only the beautiful can be that fierce, a risk,
Beatrice. You think that time is what you want,
But it is absence, the absence of duration,
Permissible in death, which will quantify
The lover and beloved—in history, too soon,
Where, of the two times, only one is counted.
Under the griffin lamppost, the youngest girl
Holds the wake of her blue dress. She has to stop herself,

The feeling is so strong: she loves, it follows
That she would explain to him who would not remember
Ever having seen her, even now. Beatrice
Wears yellow, the poet's color synonymous with light.
A sentimentalist like Halliday
Is the right choice for this picture. He would say
That beauty is a proof of incarnation, a measure
Of the artist's art. And thus desire is better

If it remain a prayer. But Dante and the blue girl
Stray: as if to lose were to stand still.

PART II

Dies Irae

Love, the preacher said, is not
A wonder of the weather. It admits,
Instead, of error—taking place in time
Which ends in judgment, as on the day
The dead convene, when it's after,
After all. You looked at me,

As if I had been chosen, and then
The scale toppled in your outstretched hand.
It was hard to tell if it was
A gift you offered or a test
To see how I would measure. I looked up
And saw, upside down, spent bodies

Being hurled, and thus I had to figure out
The story: Jesus was about to come in glory,
With a sword. Love or judgment, when
The Hell Mouth opens, the setting is a well,
Where Jacob first saw Rachel, where Rebecca, too,
Drew up stony water and placed a cup

In the stranger's hand. Water or ashes:
What fills a depth is, in time, as light
As snow, and the preacher erred: it is

A vagary of weather whether, when called,
It's up or down you go, whether
You will read the sign correctly

Or then or after, ever know.

Les Cahiers de la Malade

I

Magdalen

I unwrapped the artist's gift: a skull
In charcoal on white ground. The sky
Through that window was better left unopened.

Crisp and even were the socket-eyes
Like black keys for Saint Stephen's Day
Come now now now, the song for four small hands.

Footsteps of the *danse macabre*
Lined up in the snow. But the desert
Is the place for reparation. At the foot of the cross,

A skull is the sign for Golgotha: cursed land atoned,
From Adam's grave, the sky. Magdalen stands vigil.
She was beautiful: it was not enough to be forgiven.

She loved. And threw the glass jewels on the snow
Where Good King Wenceslaus walked out.
And saw what others saw. This was not his story.
He could not stop her. She lifted up
The alabaster jar. *Nothing is secret now*

II

Dum spiro spero.

The morning starts out in the afternoon's
Arrangements to make the next day a comfort. It's comfort,
Not truth, the invalid is after.
And if the driveway circles like a rosary—

Gray stones from an Irish shrine, it's a chain
To haul the out-of-kilter body from the bed,
Until, as well-appointed as an apparition,
She shows up, and smiles then, at her doctor,

And if she's there to bless and not
To cry out—the mystic's *gift of tears* stopped up
As if saved for a rainy day, for a melodramatic heaven,
Where the seeping water from the unaligned gutters

Couldn't stain a topographic ridge on the drywall wall.
The powdery extrusions are damp; even the residue
Is damp, as if something were trapped alive.
And when she breathes, it's in whistles that go round—

As if it were ordained already—in a panicked rafter:
The mewing voices boarded up

III

Of the white party, should mention be made?
The Liquitex guitar held up the larder:
White potatoes and marshmallow creme on a gessoed shelf
And in the bathroom a stack of Ivory soap.
The water in the scrubbed sink ran like a video emulsion.

Thinking of it, I catch the fear of being left alone
In an apartment that betrays, like the white one,
Its owner's resistance. I tell myself,
Be calm, breathe, you can control . . . but the radio next door
Goes off like guns. A killer that's aloose, a real one

On the run from Toledo where he gunned down four
And bludgeoned, maybe in Norwood, a husband and a wife
Who'd fixed him iced tea and had let him use their phone.
It's fear that ends in purity, akin to resolution,
To the point past pain and that artificial torpor

That a victim, say on a porch, will put on as a mask.

IV

The air machine is terminal, switched off and on
No speed, and only one direction—in.
Unconsidering,
The jet of medicine-tinged steam
Blows like silver jimmies
In the bottom of the balloon turret, an inverted cup.

The end of an uncharacteristic July has turned
The sycamore's stooped leaves
Transparent yellow, and down the street
Turquoise children kneel like suppliants
To unzipper firecrackers on the weedy lawn.
The explosions retain the present tense,

The imperative mood in delivery, not like
The words once in your hands
Scattered like winos' bottles,

Inert, folded in white paper, mistaken now
In the gate's whorls or under trees.

V

It is dark inside the windows of the hospital.
Music from the TV-radio tells the time.
Is this a dream, like Joachim's or Joseph's?
In the gospels, the women are there to be forgiven,
Not to dream, and yet a prophecy is one
To wake from, the corridor's light
A thin line at the door. The clear bags bubble, drip—
Roped off, your arms, enthralled.
You could not *rise and go.*

From the craggy sky, an angel hails the dreamer.
What is announced accrues a certainty. In the next panel,
Redemption: the donors kneeling downwind
From the twin miracles and the smelly cows.
The false words sound true, but it is
A Roman emendation: the story started the other way
Around. On the shores of Aulis, Iphigenia's seed
Was scattered. The Achaeans were godless,
Plundering the sacred ground.
Cassandra

Waited at the portal. She sang, she breathed
The blood that love would spill

Tempesta

after Giorgione

What is finite, by definition, will always be
less likely here. There is safety, after all,
in the ambiguity of ruin, where a man and a woman,
emptied of their expectations, are faithful
to the fact of Nature, more changeable than
the rumour of each other. This bluing landscape
supposedly muted by accretions—smoke from candles
and varnishes from later hands—restored now,
washed with underpainted—in defiance of
the academic method—light that seems to billow
from the ground, as if the earth were sacred,
not defiled, under the sky, as if a picture breathed,
on completion, in the weather of its fate: that is
the subject here, only related to what Giorgione
planned, preferring the implied chaos of the sporadic
trees to Giovanni Bellini's regulation, which had
seemed, in his teacher's hands, more natural—
that is to say "divine"—than the suspended weather,
the brooding ground, the blue-green of canal
water, lapping *le temps* as undertone—
the musk young girls give off, as they stir,
tossing twists of heavy hair, in church, say,
like Beatrice or Laura, turning to find

their missals in the pew and the boys behind them
who are breathless, rapt, and because they are
out of time, inevitably mistaken.

This woman was a beauty
even as a child, accustomed to that spurious adoration.
A "princess" in profile, discernible in weariness,
naked, except for a prayer robe over her shoulders
like Susanna's or Bathsheba's towel that does not
conceal her aging body. She offers her breast,
in this communion, to the child.

Is the soldier then the father,
peripheral as Joseph? Or like Adrastus, *he stands amazed.*
On guard, he's not expecting danger; looking toward,
not at, her, as if he'd loved her a long time
and is grateful now. His white shirt so brilliant
it eclipses the umber of his face almost composed
of the trees' shadows, but itself beautiful, proud,
for he is confident he knows the weather of the future,
as if, having once given her up, he has come to
believe in the beneficence of resignation, in time.
In X ray, the watcher is a woman standing in water,
perhaps a primal Anne or like the princess
in Fête Champêtre—pouring back, a gesture in reverse
of Rachel's at the well—the cyclical, silver water
it is hospitable to offer a stranger, too. For Wickhoff,
the watcher was Adrastus, searching for water when
he comes upon Hyspsipyle "lovely in her sorrow,"
with Opheltes at her breast, and is that the reason
he looks away: is he embarrassed by the baby's hunger?
To love is easier, less a risk, than being loved.
Love, that storm blurring distinctions—coming, will

come, not come, welcome. What becomes, for
art historians, the "subject of endless controversy,"
for Giorgione has built his story like a stanza
with a room for doubt, as if it had all happened,
in the early morning prophecy, in memory: the refuge
of an open field; the paradox of precedence; the luminous
city curving on a hill with a white dome like
Bramante's *tempietto,* though this is free Venice,
not stricken Rome, and so the idea of martyrdom
is distant, too. They know already that they
are mortal here where white tablets glimmer
in a burdened sky. A man, a woman, a child—
who would resolve that interval? That is
their privacy, their only flaw: they are unwilling—
there is time enough yet—to be comforted.

Rose Bowl

"... for the roses
Had the look of flowers that are looked at."
T. S. Eliot, "Burnt Norton," *Four Quartets*

If I hold it to my ear, the hollow sounds
like someone breathing, instead of the sea,
because the Gulf of Mexico's on all sides, already
we can hear the sea. Back for my grandmother's death,
I find the rose bowl, a Victorian *objet,* on a shelf inside
the gray room whose windowsills held stones, when
I used to live with her, of the same, indeterminate color.
The porcelain is the cloudy celadon of vellum, with minute cracks
so that it seems more fragile, like a shell. Remembering,
I look inside; it's empty: my Aunt Marion has had it cleaned
already, as if she were afraid any orifice could hold
a soul weak enough to tell its story. That night, in fact,
is Halloween; children roam Blind Pass in packs. I turn
the patio lights on and fix Aunt Marion a scotch. Our first
customer is a dark girl cocooned in Saran Wrap. She looks
like a nebulizer for an air machine. "What a costume,"
I say in doubt. "I'm Snow White, just before I got woke up.
I wanted to be Janet Jackson, she's so cool, but my mother
said it was clichéd." I offer the treats, but she nods No.
"Thanks," she says, "but I can't have candy. I just do it
for the ritual." We all turn toward the vigilant one dividing
the light at the sidewalk's end.

My grandmother was not that kind
of mother. Her children scuffled through boarding schools or,
at home, stole doughnuts for breakfast—on their own. She liked
counting money in the morning, tolerable only after a Pall Mall.
At night I would help her into her off-the-shoulder, Oscar-de-
la-Renta
spin-offs, her platinum hair roped into knob. She would stay
at the club until "last call." Now she had turned those
mahogany, smoke, and urine colors: Manhattans, diamonds,
Shalimar. Smoothed over her twiggy body was a pink
chiffon nightgown she could only have been caught dead in.
My father and Aunt Marion were the principal
greeters. My mother's and my job was to be beautiful and still.
She held my elbow; she pulled the laces taut. And when
I woke, the lid was hammered tight, and I saw the huntsman's
roses that were meant to be a sign, and the blood, too,
ticking like petals through a jar. *You are too young
to be a mother.* Mourning is its weather. *Hopeless love.*
I looked into the mirror and saw my mother.
Fair is fairest. Sand is an absolute, like snow.
She will spill, it said. *You will be spilled.*
She will will, and you, I knew it, too, will last.

Fortune

Was seclusion what we yearned for, if
The lines of perspective seem to meet in us,
And here we are: the center of a showy painting.

As if our dreams were coming closer to our lives—
With the incompleteness, the bad lighting
Of genre scenes meant to document quotidian
Oppression and the painter's art.

When we curl into the car each day,
It's for keeps; the pressure of your body bearing down

The way a cook will wrap a sliced carrot around a pencil
To make it curl—someone has wrapped your body around
A steering wheel and ordered errands due
Before a certain hour—the reckoning taken

At the sooty field spliced by a walkway and a tower
Where no birds sing, but old women at the looms—

They sound the strings, like harps.
Their earthly arms seem flawless then
In the pause before they pluck the filament—

Flax as impossible as gold—
And the letting go, like all resolutions, graceless:
Stopping the tremor of the obdurate wheel.

A Story

I

The pedestal describes what it is holding:
A gilt window and an inner door. The relic
Is the martyr's heart the skeptic can't believe in.
It has been parcelled out and now is small.
Between the upraised hand and the seedpod
Curved because it is a sword, we were called;
It was a calling. The gun-metal ships
At anchor on the horizon, in Florida
Where only the weather happens. You said Maybe and I said
No and then you turned away from me and we walked
Deliberately from the concave sky, confused by sand,
Past sea oats protected by a sign, we hurried
To your practical car, and then we saw, near
The beach shower, a cormorant, so still.
Her sideways eyes looked crusted, the fishing line
Clotted in filigree around her bloodied beak.
You took the backseat towel, you crouched,
Walking on your knees, and I drove the three blocks
To my grandmother's house where the useless fireplace
Was clouded by a mirror and we could see the porcelain
Ladies in postures of reluctance and the chairs of ghosts.

II

The houses are still two-tone, but different colors
Behind the too-pruned royal palms and the rank oleander.
Someone has misconstrued, reading cessation for desire:
The unrelenting pebble driveways banked by razor-blade yuccas
Whose blooms are eggs that do not rot or fall. This is the end
Of the exigent—the perpetual, unvarying ratio
Of sky to water. If the beach erodes, they dredge
It in again. And I tell the story over, as I understand it,
Over time: because it was holy, it would not burn;
Because the sun increases on the side of mercy *ever*
Never, quantifying duration toward *always*
At the fictive shore, where the pool boy and the surgeon
Time-share the job of cosmetic reconstruction, where
You said you could outwait me, far from where I know
What it is to live in time and to forgive.

Erinnerung

Telemann, the trumpet leaves that are Naples yellow billow
onto Payne's gray stone, onto the mound of antique letters
in out-of-fashion colors: ochre, chromium, sienna brown.
In an attic box I find one I didn't send. To open it
I have to break the adolescent, ageratum seal. The writer
  described
herself, "child of a disgraced father," among her books—
Virgil and Shakespeare, Trigonometry because it was required,
while across the street, Conti's Italian Restaurant's neon
blinked in the continual suspension that was Florida—
the harmonic air dank with salt and jasmine, as if it had
been exhaled, while the grandmother took the white Cadillac
(25 mph) to St. John's for Bingo, and the upstairs tenant,
the retired retailer, paced to and fro between the narrow beds,
and the smothered sounds of gulls arising from the clayey sand
were followed by the roar from "The Locker," the nightclub
next door, when the "he-shes" at midnight ripped off
their Barbie-doll wigs and bowed, showing their cleavage.
For it was a mystery, *requirito,* to keep on asking after,
the feminine, *myein,* how it was disdained, but on holidays
to be acquired, at Notre Dame Academy, whose lime green walls
smelled of hair spray and of extra esters released from
S. Pierre Marie's erratic lab. They were beautiful, the sisters,
in mufti—as thin as runway models and festive, as if their lives

were done. It was palpable, the sense, not despairing, of *after,* Arden, errata. (They left the convent the next year.) *A child you were when first I beheld you.* Who loved her (dux ego vester eram) they all said they did, when she lived on Gulf Boulevard and wrote letters, Aliena, then.

PART III

Postulant

Leonardo's *Annunciation*

It is *gravitas,* the gray of quarry stone, the burden
of the middle plane, the *moving toward* the heavy hour
the angels come, bearing grief whose name is benediction.
The beauty here is of ornament—the lectern, the cassone—
both calculations. The trees, serialized, the lilies limned with
gilt,
as if Leonardo had copied an exercise from his notebook, the
flowers
have the aridity of the secondhand, for what is more
melancholy
than exactitude, the graphite stick's precision that imitates
the economy of doubt: *it is so small it can be used again.*

The balustrade divides the plane in half: the negative space
like dark water that stops the heart of the one
who looks the longest down, because between duty
and inspiration is a wall, between the heart and its desires,
and obfuscation, so the work is flawless, hence oblique,
no incarnation. It records, instead, the scrutiny
of exactly how one failed *in Verrocchio's studio, over time*—
propped against the wall and taken out
to be looked at and to do again.

For it's not a gift if it's asked for. *The lowliest*
of his servants was simple, saying Yes, yet she was troubled
How can this be? But he was more comfortable with misgiving
and so the paint's application is scrupulous
not Fra Angelico daubing the transparent color wet on wet
but a man *because song was denied him*
who drew, speaking not of grace and its lambent color
but of work, of working through the half-tone
that announces the grievous half-time, the pause
in the plainsong—how the soul strives
to magnify the Lord by growing small, and because
It sufficeth not, the postulant, in chorus,
claims, stretching forth a hand.

The viewer, too, is outside the composition—
reading the metaphor of the garden that was closed.
Dressed already in gray and umber, she looks up from her
weaving:
she is not surprised. *God is my strength* welcomes Mary
to her work which was *to know* the bitter
plainness, the plaintiveness
of restitution: the gray overwrought to black:
the word made death so it could dwell among us.

To Be Childless Is an Error?

I

There's a sky with nothing in it—
No parachute, as if to save you,
Has buckled from the empty ceiling:

Your nieces must be taken to the zoo;
Their voices are squeaky, like vermilion cellophane.

The hill to the antelopes you storm, but their shoes
Are wrong for such an outing: the straps will bind
Their webby toes, unless you accede and wheel—

They're not embarrassed—those grimy, rented strollers.
And you yourself are old enough for comfort—

It is not right to hate these stubborn children.

II

In a lilac room, I hold a red-haired child.
Through the open door, I watch women in the black of visitors
Separate, go still.

I think it is my mother's baby from twenty years ago.
Outside the schoolroom a bulldozer had tracked furrows,
Zigzag of tombstones on a hill.

When I look back, I am alone.
I sort through dresser drawers, through plastic bags
Of arms and legs—for dolls, I think.

If she's still alive, she'll cry.
But dangling from the last bag, like a twist-closed wire,
A note: *Silent, the child has grown to be like you.*

I turn then to the empty door. Bunched like nodules
At the base of ferns, the women's thin breasts swell.
How will I tell, I think, until I am afraid to ask them.

Where the child is, what we look like, if they know.

III

A spray of white water emptied from a vat:
Sewage being spread apart and cleaned: Such are
My dreams! On the other side of the harbor, a tide pool
Where the pregnant women, their heads bowed,
Walk in twos and threes.

They are fair-haired in lilac dresses.
Through the faded cotton, their stomachs seem to pulse.
Why are they walking, holding one another's hands?
Nothing can live here; the floor is filled with coins
Leftover from a dead man's eyes. I who want to join them,

To walk barefoot, back and forth, expecting nothing,
Wait my turn, until I, too, sink, into the water;
I hold my breath—afraid its rush will draw me
In the wrong direction. There is nothing to seize hold of,
And I breathe—I have to—and taste the reeking water.

When I rise, farther than ever from the crowded shore,
My grandmother's body floats past me like a raft.
Her swollen fingers flash their rings.
I study her stomach, which is flat and puckered.
"What have you done with them?" I ask.

Charing Cross

Inside our bookish flat in Pimlico
Its cupboards bare with only canisters of
India-ink tea amid stacks of laminated place mats—
Burnt circles occluding Buckingham Palace
And the Tower, I study the walls askew with photographs
Of Archie Cotterell, our landlords' son—his teams,
The diffident succession of each year.

Sometimes we walk the Thames's bleak corridors
To the Rothkos, the idea of the burnished, ostensive
Border as a river that bleeds and is unhoused,
Or I brave the chartered wind, boarding a red bus
For my pilgrimage, off Trafalgar Square,
Toward Leonardo—the ghosts of Mary and her mother,
The X-ray–revealed cartoon incised into a shroud.

On the way back, I buy what I can carry
Always the gods give small gifts to the small
Shifting *The Times* to accommodate the sprouts
In my string bag, solving, out of habit, the streets'
Parallel equations toward the station's stairs—
The horizontal door, where I almost step on
A crouching beggar, the YOU ARE HERE sign

Pointing downward to the gessoed spikes
Of her red hair. She seems too shy to have
Asked anyone for money; she asks me, then jangles
Like a gypsy but in black redolent of Shalimar
To duck beneath the jagged turnstiles.
"I'll be OK," she calls. "I know where I'm going."
And I know who I love—if and only if *ostinato*

The condition repeats because it isn't true—
She measured her love to show him
Go in and out the window
She followed him to London
Where is he going now, he was going with her
As we have gone before—
The one the dear Lord knew she wouldn't marry.

A Potter's Wheel

A bowl finds its inescapable
application in the rigor of
its sides that, starting, have to end
as smaller, more confined, where the
end starts up again, like the hypnotist's
wheel in '50's movies; one piebald
frame following another so that
it is a story by virtue of
the quick proximity of its parts:
to be close to one and to one
another day by day around a
dinner table, for example, years
in place (with the same cutlery,
the same tried recipes, only
flowers fresh that day); that is
a sequence that can tell the simple
story—how gravity decrees
that what is close gets closer,
tighter, drawing toward its middle
which ends up as its end—this
unwound, this concentrated
absence which, Sunday nights,
through the years we occupy,
calmly knowing absence is what
connects a circle to its frame

and makes it then a story, explicable
as we who are told and telling
come quickly to the end which is to
be laid waste—starting up in
circles again, until it seems
by virtue of necessity that we
are or should by now be filled

The Birth of the Virgin

I

The childless are not at home in any weather:
they are always cold. Too early for the Uffizi,
we creep into Santa Maria Novella and interrupt a Mass.
The cavernous *chiesa* is aglow with votive candles
that a stocking-capped old woman sells, in the foyer,
from a box, and the murmurous hum of women
praying for their apostate sons. At the bottom of the story
cycle behind the altar, Joachim is driven from the temple
that was, for the young men, a cupola of trees. The lamb
he tried to offer scrambles up rocks as toothed
as lunar mountains—where Joachim, in the far right
of the future, sleeps—the habitual escape from shame,
and less of a surprise than good fortune, always new
enough to be announced. The angel in the red cloud
looks just like a lightbulb thought; he blows a tiny horn
as the old man wakes, staggered like a staircase
on a staircase mountain. Off to the darker side, Anna
greets her husband. The attendant women look away:
do they think that it's unseemly—the lavishness of joy:
two old people who should be used to one another.
Life-size, at eye-level, as if this were the present tense,
where we live, important to one another, though we cannot
have a child. The Golden Gate hardly matters, except
in the retelling. It isn't gold at all.

II

How easy is the working out of grace! Above the young priest's head,
Anna leans on an elbow in the posture of Etruscan sarcophagi,
only she is alone, and this is not a coffin, but a birthing bed.
Her attendant women, placed on two planes, are ceremonious
in gold and ivory gowns; they look at us. The *Blue Guide*
gives their names: the Tornabuoni heiresses who would die,
the year after, in pregnancy or of the plague.

III

Back home in Cincinnati, the right-to-lifers parade,
like pages trailing ticker tape, on the stock market's floor,
only they are fat and poor, these presidents of Holy Name clubs—
in T-shirts and ball caps, pushing strollers. Before
the court injunction they would crouch behind a planter, then
  spring,
when a young girl, as in the Presentation, would mount the
  Jacob's
ladder to the clinic's portico. One cried, falsetto, "Don't kill
me, Mama!" The others raised their fists; they yelled, "Hitler,
Baby-killer, Tramp!" Alone of all her sex—they said of her—
Mary lacked concupiscence, and thus could say No only to
temptation: which accounts, in part, for her humiliation—
steadfast at the foot of the cross or enthroned—modest
among men in triptychs ground in gold, flanked by John the
  Baptist,
crazed and haggard—a mirror to the one who was only sin
  and love,
Magdalen, who, too, said always Yes, but now holds the temple
of her body—a gold Pandora's jar that tells that "after"
is always longer than "before." The ironic *immaculata*—

the repentant, the other Mary. Neither one could be a priest
whose job is judgment, for *she would be ruled, and in sorrow.*
In Giovanni Bellini's *Madonna of the Meadow,* the raven
is a signpost in the laden, blue lake of the sky. Mary
is an old woman who holds a baby boy akimbo; he is clay-
  colored,
as if she had wanted him to die, before the cross, within
her body, twisted like a nail. *And in sorrow shall she not.*
The attendant women wear green T-shirts so that the clients
will not be confused. It is Hildegarde's green, signifying
plenitude. They bear each other's bodies on the steps
of the temple, at the threshold of the clinic's door.

Achill

The hill was stained-glass, I remember that.
The sky, that bereaved color of yellowing paper.
The high windows were soldered with shells, as if in offering.

The sea, of course, was at the bottom of the promontory,
continuous, contrived.
So we were *by the water:* that was the composition's tonal key.
The clear blue radiating from below the horizon, signifying
absolution
For that early error *lest we start another journey.*
(It is not we who start the journey.)
The gate again was closed,
so we walked around the ambulatory

Toward the Stations of the Cross, mosaics pressed into
the sea-foam marble wall: a door implied, a window emptied
in the last rays of the stagnant light, *toward England,* the
imperium,
for language is the onus of our exile, and the work,
as well: to fold our hands at the wrist and rest, *no longer
keeping
everything within.* The soul departs the body, *lepidoptera*
through the mouth. *Macroglossum stellatarum*

Migrates toward the starry light, toward ornate weather.
Because you hearkened to the voice of your wife, cursed be the ground.
When the sacristan holds the taper, the windows darken.

YWH

The syllables in the name of God
Are suitably suppressed. You have to know
To know: the principle of faith, or is it language?
In the crowded Clifton Library, where it smells
Of steamy wool and cough drops, still in basic black
I crouch in the corner pocket, near the 929.8s
Sidling past the khaki-wrapped street person
Who looks up from the unfurled *NYT*
And nods to me, as I, holding my breath, pull down

What to Name Your Baby. Do I know
Him, already knowing the good ones invoke
The Lord who is salvation, which becomes
The namer's own, or they betoken gratitude
For gracious gifts, and it is just,
If it's a son. Desolate, I nod back, convinced
I'll choose the name his mother did the research for—
Perhaps the one Zacharias wrote upon the tablet
Before his tongue was loosened, *John,*
Whose mother, Elisabeth, had believed
That the future in her would be performed.

Gabriel comes in flames, not meekly, in flames
Buoyed up by blood, but the daughters come
Unbidden; they fill in, until as mothers

They are recognized; their sons, announced.
I have seen this one scan the trash and raise
An orange carton so that the milk flowed down
His matted beard. Who cannot believe in signs?
Did he once suck of her body who will now mourn
Make ready the way of the Lord
Because she could not, in the end, provide?

Apparition

At Mount Storm, the migrating Monarchs
Brush past the children's ears—causing havoc
And shrill cries: "It's a bee!" The children
Feel as if they're in control if they seek to flee.
When they bolt into the parking lot, they block my body
Unless you bless, with blunt fists in my thigh. That night,

I dream the basilica again, the groin vault's early Gothic
Gray that repeats the sky's secret of proportion: how
It can be used to market the sacred and its end. The indigo
Window above the altar is held open by a ladder chain
Which is eternity. And the clerestory's yellow fleurs-de-lis
Look like butterflies seeking colder weather, where

You appear, a breath made visible in the tomby air.
You say what was never given you, your name. And when
I wake, next to my daughter, it is too late. I need to use
My asthma spray. Rising from the ashen ground, the voices
Of the host of children, in the dark, in single file
Lest they be smited on their way to school.

Notes

The collection's title invokes John Donne's poem "Air and Angels."

"The Wood of Error" reimagines Canto I of the *Inferno* (Dante's *Commedia*).

"The Meeting of Dante and Beatrice" is an ecphrasis of Henry Holliday's painting in the Walker Art Gallery (Liverpool, England).

"Erinnerung" quotes Virgil's *Eclogue 8;* the parenthetical clause, as translated by C. Day Lewis, is: "I took charge of you." (*The Eclogues and Georgics of Virgil,* New York: Anchor Books, 1964, pp. 58–59.)

The penultimate stanza of **"Charing Cross"** makes use of a Scottish ballad, "I Know Where I'm Going"; the final stanza quotes another traditional song, "Go In and Out the Window."

The James Dickey Contemporary Poetry Series
Edited by Richard Howard

Error and Angels
Maureen Bloomfield

Portrait in a Spoon
James Cummins

The Land of Milk and Honey
Sarah Getty

All Clear
Robert Hahn

Traveling in Notions:
The Stories of Gordon Penn
Michael J. Rosen

United Artists
S. X. Rosenstock